A Journal for Using

THE CREATIVE CURRICULUM®
for Infants&
Toddlers

_____

Name

Amy Laura Dombro ❖ Laura J. Colker ❖ Diane Trister Dodge

TEACHING STRATEGIES INC.

ISBN: 1-879537-34-6
Library of Congress Catalog Card Number: 97-62074

Published by:
Teaching Strategies, Inc.
P.O. Box 42243
Washington, DC 20015

Distributed by:
Gryphon House
P.O. Box 207
Beltsville, MD 20704-0207

Graphic design:
Amy Wajda

Illustrations:
Jennifer Barrett O'Connell

Acknowledgments:
The first draft of the Journal was reviewed in August 1997 by participants at our Staff Development Conference. We are indebted to them and also to Sherrie Rudick, Sarah Minteer Semlak, Costella Tate, Rachel Theilheimer, and Ruth Uhlmann for their very constructive and thoughtful suggestions. We thank Judith Leipzig for the questions on building trust. The idea for a community map came from John P. Kretzmann and John L. McKnight in *Building Communities from the Inside Out: A Path towards Finding and Mobilizing a Community's Assets* (Evanston, IL: Center for Urban Affairs and Policy Research). Finally, we thank Toni Bickart for helping to edit and proof the final draft.

Contents

Getting Started

This Journal is about you and the very important work you do. You may work with children and families in a center-based program or in your home. You may be experienced or new to caring for infants and toddlers. You may have just opened *The Creative Curriculum for Infants & Toddlers* or you may have been using it for a while. No matter where you are in your career, we hope this Journal will confirm what you know about caring for infants and toddlers. We also hope it will give you new ideas and strategies for improving your program.

The Journal goes through the Curriculum chapter by chapter, asking you to relate what you learn to your own situation. Icons, such as the one at the right, and margin notes guide you through the process. Step-by-step, we will help you try out new ideas and reflect on your work.

Chapter
1
pages 23–30

The Journal can serve as the basis of discussion at staff meetings or family child care association meetings, in courses, or one-on-one dialogues with colleagues or a mentor. Some of the information you collect, such as observations of children, may be useful in parent conferences. You may want to go through the Journal from beginning to end, or concentrate on sections that relate to areas of your program you have a question about or you want to improve. We recommend, however, that everyone begin with pages 3–17, which focus on you and set the stage for everything that follows.

Keep in mind that creating and maintaining a quality program for infants and toddlers is an ongoing journey, not a task you— or anyone else—can accomplish and cross off as "done." You may spend several months or even a year going through the Journal. As you do, celebrate the things you do well and the many strengths you bring to your work. Face the tough questions and remember that every day you work with children and families you learn more.

Why a Curriculum for Infants and Toddlers?

In making the decision to write *The Creative Curriculum for Infants & Toddlers,* we carefully considered whether such a curriculum was really necessary. After all, if a good quality program is about building relationships and making the most of everyday routines and activities, why would you need a curriculum to guide your work?

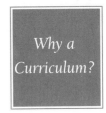

Why a Curriculum?

pages 1–18

As you begin this Journal, we ask you to consider this same question. First, think about what you do every day as you care for infants and toddlers.

Pick out just five of the many responsibilities you juggle on a daily basis and list them below.

_____

_____

_____

_____

_____

_____

In the introductory chapter to *The Creative Curriculum for Infants & Toddlers,* we walk you through a typical day. You will probably find many, if not all, of the responsibilities you listed above. In the margin notes, we explain why these daily tasks are important for children's development and the role that each plays in a curriculum. We also identify the chapters where you will find these tasks discussed.

Read pages 9–14, which describe "A Typical Day."

We believe that being aware of *why* you do what you do will help you make sure that your everyday decisions add up to a quality program. Like curriculum for older children, *The Creative Curriculum for Infants & Toddlers* gives you a plan of where, what, and how to guide children's learning.

So, to answer our initial question, a curriculum for infants and toddlers gives you the framework you need for making the everyday decisions that add up to quality. In graphic terms, the Curriculum looks like this:

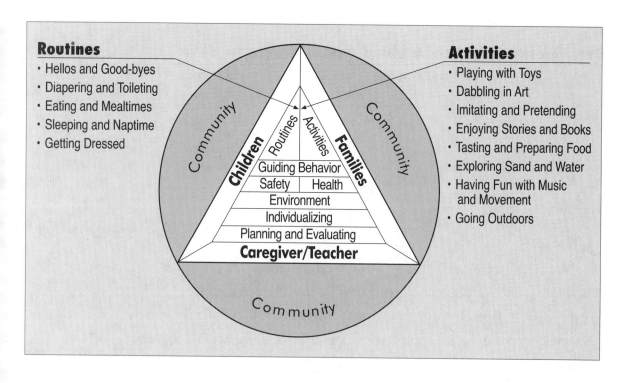

Focusing on You: The Key to Quality

Look once again at the curriculum triangle. It shows that you are at the foundation of the program. This is because you are responsible for building the relationships that are the focus of the curriculum. We give you the title "caregiver/teacher."

What is your title at work?

_____

How does the title "caregiver/teacher" fit with how you see your role?

_____

_____

_____

_____

_____

_____

_____

_____

Looking at Your Professional Development

Let's keep the focus on you a while longer. In the framed area below, draw a map of your career path. Use words, symbols, or pictures. Your map can be as simple or as complex as you'd like. It should, however, include the following three points:

• where you began your work with children
• where you see yourself today
• where you think you would like to be five years from now

As you look at the map you drew of your career path, think about the following questions:

What led you to work with infants and toddlers?

_____

_____

_____

_____

Have your reasons for working with infants and toddlers changed over time? If so, how?

_____

_____

_____

_____

What do you like best about your work with children under three and their families?

_____

_____

_____

_____

What is the hardest thing about your work?

_____

_____

_____

_____

Wherever you are on your career path, your personality, values, interests, knowledge, and sense of humor make your program unlike any other. For example, if you love to cook, chances are the children you work with have many experiences peeling bananas, spreading apple butter on bread, and stirring pancake batter.

What are your special strengths and interests?

_____

_____

_____

_____

_____

_____

_____

_____

How might *The Creative Curriculum for Infants & Toddlers* help you to share these interests with children and families?

_____

_____

_____

_____

_____

_____

_____

_____

Assessing Your Personal Goals and Objectives

It is a myth that anyone can take care of infants and toddlers. To create a quality program, you need special skills and knowledge. In *The Creative Curriculum for Infants & Toddlers* we have identified six important areas:

- building responsive relationships

- planning and managing a developmentally appropriate program

- promoting children's development and learning

- continuing to learn about children, families, and the field of early childhood education

- maintaining professional standards

- advocating in support of children and families

In the next six pages we present a self-assessment tool you can use. It will help you identify the goals and objectives you would like to work on as you implement the Curriculum.

Self-Assessment:
Goals and Objectives for Caregivers/Teachers

Caregiver/Teacher:_____ **Date completed:**_____

Directions: Read each goal and objective. To rate yourself on each objective, circle the appropriate number. On the lines following the word *Comments,* give examples that explain why you rated yourself the way you did. To help you get started, see the examples for each objective in Appendix A, pages 321–326.

Goal 1: To build responsive relationships

Objective:	To form positive, trusting relationships with children
RATING	*Comments:*

5 HIGH

4

3

2

1 LOW

_____

_____

_____

_____

_____

Objective:	To form positive relationships with families to support children's growth and development
RATING	*Comments:*

5 HIGH

4

3

2

1 LOW

_____

_____

_____

_____

_____

Goal 1: To build responsive relationships (continued)

Objective:

RATING

5	HIGH
4	
3	↑
2	
1	LOW

To work with colleagues and community representatives to support children and families

Comments:

_____

_____

_____

_____

_____

Goal 2: To plan and manage a developmentally appropriate program

Objective:

RATING

5	HIGH
4	
3	↑
2	
1	LOW

To plan and evaluate a program that meets the needs of the children and families served

Comments:

_____

_____

_____

_____

_____

Objective:

RATING

5	HIGH
4	
3	↑
2	
1	LOW

To observe children regularly and individualize the program based on these observations

Comments:

_____

_____

_____

_____

_____

Goal 2: To plan and manage a developmentally appropriate program (continued)

Objective: **To create a warm and welcoming environment that supports children's growth and development**

RATING

5	HIGH
4	
3	↑
2	
1	LOW

Comments:

_____
_____
_____
_____
_____

Objective: **To ensure the safety of children in the program**

RATING

5	HIGH
4	
3	↑
2	
1	LOW

Comments:

_____
_____
_____
_____
_____

Objective: **To ensure the health of children in the program**

RATING

5	HIGH
4	
3	↑
2	
1	LOW

Comments:

_____
_____
_____
_____
_____

Objective: **To guide children's behavior in positive ways**

RATING

5	HIGH
4	
3	↑
2	
1	LOW

Comments:

_____
_____
_____
_____
_____

Goal 3: To promote children's development and learning

Objective:	To use routines as opportunities for growth and learning

RATING

5   HIGH
4
3   ↑
2
1   LOW

Comments:

_____
_____
_____
_____
_____

Objective:	To provide activities that will facilitate children's growth and development

RATING

5   HIGH
4
3   ↑
2
1   LOW

Comments:

_____
_____
_____
_____
_____

Goal 4: To continue learning about children, families, and the field of early childhood education

Objective:	To participate in training to expand skills and knowledge

RATING

5   HIGH
4
3   ↑
2
1   LOW

Comments:

_____
_____
_____
_____
_____

Objective:	To participate in professional early childhood education organizations

RATING

5   HIGH
4
3   ↑
2
1   LOW

Comments:

_____
_____
_____
_____
_____

Goal 4: To continue learning about children, families and the field of early childhood education (continued)

Objective:

RATING

5	HIGH
4	↑
3	
2	
1	LOW

To observe colleagues to learn new successful techniques and approaches

Comments:

_____
_____
_____
_____
_____
_____

Goal 5: To maintain professional standards

Objective:

RATING

5	HIGH
4	↑
3	
2	
1	LOW

To be ethical in all dealings with children, families, and community representatives

Comments:

_____
_____
_____
_____
_____
_____

Objective:

RATING

5	HIGH
4	↑
3	
2	
1	LOW

To respect the privacy and confidentiality of children and parents

Comments:

_____
_____
_____
_____
_____
_____

Goal 5: To maintain professional standards (continued)

Objective:

To demonstrate respect for all children and families

Comments:

RATING

5	HIGH
4	
3	↑
2	
1	LOW

_____
_____
_____
_____
_____

Goal 6: To be an advocate in support of children and families

Objective:

To educate others about the need for high standards and quality programs

Comments:

RATING

5	HIGH
4	
3	↑
2	
1	LOW

_____
_____
_____
_____
_____

Objective:

To work with community agencies in support of children and families

Comments:

RATING

5	HIGH
4	
3	↑
2	
1	LOW

_____
_____
_____
_____

After completing the self-assessment, think about the following questions:

What are your greatest strengths?

_____

_____

_____

_____

_____

_____

_____

_____

_____

_____

What do you think your colleagues or the children's families would view as your greatest strengths?

_____

_____

_____

_____

_____

_____

_____

_____

_____

In what areas would you like to make changes?

_____

_____

_____

_____

_____

_____

_____

How might you get information or develop the skills you need to make changes?

_____

_____

_____

_____

_____

_____

_____

For example, you might focus on sections of the Curriculum that address these needs, observe and talk with colleagues, read an article or book, attend workshops or take a class offered in your community.

Part
I Who's Who
in a Quality Program

In quality programs, trusting responsive relationships exist among the key players: families, children, and caregivers/teachers. Because programs exist within communities, relationships must be established with key agencies. You play a central role in nurturing these relationships. The infants and toddlers you care for are learning about who they are as people. How you relate to them affects how they feel about themselves and others. Children are part of families, and good relationships with families are critical to the success of your program. Because families may look to you to guide them to other resources in the community, you need to be familiar with the services in your community.

Building Relationships: The Focus of Your Work

Children begin learning who they are and how to relate to other people through their relationships with the important people in their lives. Research has shown that trusting responsive relationships between children and their caregivers/teachers are at the core of quality care. Having a primary caregiver—someone who will be there to care for them every day—helps children feel secure. Your relationship provides children with a "home base." They are able to explore and to get to know the other people and things in their environment, secure in the knowledge they can always come "home" to you.

Chapter

1

pages 23–30

Let's think for a minute about what it takes to build relationships. Think about someone you know whom you trust.

How do you feel when you are with that person?

_____

_____

_____

What characteristics about that person make you feel safe and secure?

_____

_____

_____

Think about your own similar qualities. (Don't be modest.)

What do you do to encourage children and families to trust you?

_____

_____

_____

_____

_____

_____

Building Relationships with Children

Pages 24 and 25 list strategies for building relationships with children.

As you read through the strategies for building relationships with children, think about the children in your program.

Why is it easier to build relationships with some children than with others?

_____

_____

_____

_____

_____

_____

It sometimes requires a special effort on your part to make a relationship work.

What characteristics of a child make it difficult for you to establish a positive relationship?

What steps do you take to build a positive relationship with all children?

Building Relationships with Families

Children need you and their families to work together. By doing so, you each get to know a child better than either of you could on your own.

Think about a particular child in your group.

What have you helped this child's parents learn about their child?

_____

_____

_____

_____

_____

_____

What is something you have learned about the child from the parents?

_____

_____

_____

_____

_____

_____

_____

You are the bridge between a child's two worlds: home and child care. Yet even in the best of relationships, there may be times you and families disagree about something. Though you both want the best for a child, you may have different ideas of how and when to get there.

Review the strategies for resolving differences on pages 29–30.

Think of a time you and a family have disagreed about something.

What did you disagree about?

_____

_____

_____

_____

_____

_____

_____

_____

How did you resolve your differences?

_____

_____

_____

_____

_____

_____

_____

_____

What did you learn about the child and family from this experience?

_____

_____

_____

_____

_____

_____

_____

_____

_____

What did you learn about yourself?

_____

_____

_____

_____

_____

_____

_____

_____

Knowing Infants and Toddlers

All curriculum planning begins with knowing children. In order to make good decisions, you have to know how infants and toddlers grow and develop. Chapter 2 describes infant/toddler development and how children differ in temperament and special needs.

Chapter

2

pages 31–44

After reading the chapter, think about one child in your program. Look through that child's eyes to answer the following questions.

What is this child currently learning about:

him or herself?

_____

_____

_____

_____

Refer to the charts Individualizing Goals and Objectives for Young Infants, Mobile Infants, or Toddlers *in Appendix B to help you think about a child's development. Pages 31–40 will give you more information.*

his or her feelings?

_____

_____

_____

_____

_____

What is this child currently learning about:

other people?

_____

_____

_____

_____

communicating?

_____

_____

_____

_____

moving and doing?

_____

_____

_____

thinking?

_____

_____

_____

_____

Recognizing a Child's Individuality

Keep in mind that children don't fall into neat categories. Each has a unique personality.

See page 40 for a list of characteristics that show how each child is different.

What interests, needs, and learning styles make this child different from other children in your program?

_____

_____

_____

_____

_____

_____

Children are also born with unique temperaments. Being aware of a child's temperament can sometimes help you to understand his or her behavior.

See page 41 for a discussion of temperament.

How would you describe this child's temperament? Is this child generally flexible? Cautious or fearful? Feisty, active, or intense?

_____

_____

_____

_____

_____

_____

How will you use this information to care for this child?

_____

_____

_____

_____

_____

_____

Children with Special Needs

Pages 42–44 are about working with children and families with special needs. There is information about the federal legislation on infants and toddlers with disabilities (Part C).

Are you currently working with a child who has special needs? If not, one day you probably will. Children with disabilities need to have the same opportunities as all children.

What are your feelings about caring for a child with special needs?

_____

_____

_____

_____

_____

_____

_____

How does (would) a child with special needs benefit from being in your program?

_____

_____

_____

_____

_____

_____

How do (would) you meet the needs of a child with a disability without neglecting the needs of the rest of the children?

_____

_____

_____

_____

_____

_____

To best serve a child with a disability, you need support. Support may take many forms. You may need to obtain a piece of special equipment or arrange for an extra pair of hands at certain times of the day. It is always best to learn more about the particular disability.

See Appendix E, pages 365–367, for a list of Intervention Resources in your state.

Knowing Families

The relationship you have with each child's family, and how you support that family's relationship with their child, are very important parts of your work. The more you know about families, the better you can meet their needs.

Chapter **3** *pages 45–54*

If you have children of your own, you may remember what it was like when you first became a parent. If you do not, try to imagine what it is like to suddenly be responsible for another human being.

What kinds of feelings might new parents be experiencing?

_____

_____

_____

Parents—like their children and you—are growing and changing. After reading the three stages of development in *The Creative Curriculum for Infants & Toddlers,* think about the parents in your program.

Pages 45–47 describe three stages of development that commonly apply to parents with children under three.

How does understanding the stages parents are going through affect how you relate to them?

_____

_____

_____

_____

Read about the special concerns of families with children under three on pages 48–49.

Choose a parent (or guardian) of one of the children in your program to interview. Depending on your comfort level, you may choose someone you know well. Or you may decide to use this as an opportunity to get to know someone better. Find a half-hour or so when you can talk without interruption.

Use or adapt the following questions for your interview.

What is the most wonderful part of being a parent?

_____

_____

_____

_____

_____

What is the most challenging part for you?

_____

_____

_____

_____

What concerns do you have about having your child in child care?

_____

_____

_____

_____

What can we do to reduce your worries?

_____

_____

_____

_____

_____

What kinds of things do you want to know about your child's day when you come to pick him/her up?

_____

_____

_____

_____

_____

After completing the interview, think about what you learned.

How will this information help you in your work?

_____

_____

_____

_____

_____

_____

_____

_____

Understanding the Influence of Culture

See pages 50–52 for a discussion about culture.

Our culture influences every part of our lives—for example, the languages we speak, our feelings about what and how neatly children should eat, and even how much noise children should make. We learn about culture by living it.

Think back to your own childhood.

How did your parents and other family members react when children cried?

_____

_____

_____

_____

_____

_____

How did they express their anger?

_____

_____

_____

_____

_____

_____

_____

How did they express affection?

Who made the decisions about children?

Were boys treated the same way as girls?

What kind of discipline was used?

_____

_____

_____

_____

_____

After thinking about your answers, how do these childhood experiences influence how you work with children today?

_____

_____

_____

_____

_____

_____

Children's families can teach you a lot about their beliefs.

You can use the questions on page 50 to begin a dialogue with families about culture.

What have you learned about the values and practices of the families you serve?

_____

_____

_____

_____

_____

How does your program reflect these values and practices?

_____

_____

_____

_____

_____

_____

_____

Sometimes a family's beliefs or practices may differ from what you believe to be developmentally appropriate and best for children. For example, family-style dining can sometimes be an issue. In some cultures, children—especially boys—are discouraged from feeding themselves.

See the bottom of page 51 for another example.

Think of a situation in which a family's beliefs or practices differed from what you do in your program

Describe the situation and how you handled it.

_____

_____

_____

_____

_____

_____

_____

_____

Involving the Men in Children's Lives

See pages 52–53 for a discussion of some reasons men may be overlooked and strategies for involving men.

A quality program needs to involve everyone who is important in children's lives. Yet, for many reasons, men are often overlooked. Take time to examine your feelings about involving men in your program. You may find some feelings you didn't even know you had, even if you are a man.

What role do you think men should play in child care (e.g., should they change diapers, feed babies)?

_____

_____

_____

_____

_____

_____

Take a hard look at yourself.

What steps do you take to involve men in your program?

_____

_____

_____

_____

_____

_____

Select a father or other male member of one of the families you currently serve. (You may choose the parent interviewed earlier or select someone else.) Spend 10–15 minutes interviewing him. Adapt the following questions if you wish.

Is this a "male-friendly" place?

_____

_____

_____

_____

_____

_____

_____

What could we do to make you—and other men—feel more welcome?

_____

_____

_____

_____

_____

_____

_____

_____

In what additional ways would you like to be involved in the program?

_____

_____

_____

_____

_____

_____

_____

What did you learn from this interview to help you involve men in your program?

_____

_____

_____

_____

_____

_____

_____

_____

_____

Community: Building a Network of Support

The relationship between your program and your community is a two-way street. You provide a service that makes your community a better place for children and families. Your community has resources that can enrich your program.

pages 55–60

On the next page, draw a map of your community showing individuals or agencies that offer services for families—including your program. Once you've drawn your map, do the following.

- Draw lines between your program and your current community partners. These may include the public library where you borrow books for children to read, the community center where you give parent education classes, or the physical therapist who comes to work with a child in your setting.

- Identify resources in the community with which you don't yet have a connection but think you should.

- List additional resources you need or want to investigate.

A Map of Community Resources

As you look at your map and the community partners you have so far, you may be surprised at how much you and your program give to your community and how you benefit as well.

What specific services do you and your program provide for your community?

See page 58 for a brief discussion of what child care programs have to offer.

_____

_____

_____

_____

_____

What resources do you need from your community?

_____

_____

_____

_____

_____

How will you use these resources?

_____

_____

_____

_____

See pages 59–60 for strategies for getting involved and building new community partners.

How might you establish new community partners to help you get these needed resources?

_____

_____

_____

_____

_____

_____

Part
II The Big Picture
Putting Quality into Action

When you open a curriculum guide, do you expect to see many ideas for routines and activities? Before dealing directly with routines and activities, however, we believe it's important to first set the stage for

learning. Lots of planning goes into creating a quality program. To meet each child's needs you have to observe children and have a way to track their growth and development. The environment must be comfortable and well-organized so you have the energy to nurture infants and toddlers in an unhurried way. Safety and health concerns are priorities for families and for anyone working with young children. And finally, as children grow and become more independent, you want to have a way to guide their behavior in positive ways. These aspects of a quality program are addressed in Part II of *The Creative Curriculum for Infants & Toddlers*.

Planning and Evaluating Your Program

Planning and evaluation go hand in hand in a quality program. A plan shows you where you are going. It gives you a big picture of what you want to accomplish.

Chapter **5** *pages 65–80*

Evaluation can take many forms, including observing children and caregivers, using a standardized instrument, and interviewing parents and colleagues. Through these different types of evaluation, you can learn if your plan is working and gain information to help you make changes if necessary.

Defining Program Goals and Objectives

The underlying principle of *The Creative Curriculum for Infants & Toddlers* is that the strong relationships you build with the children and families in your program help children to grow and develop. We have set goals for working with both groups that reflect accepted standards for quality.

Review the goals for children on page 67 and the goals for working with families on page 68.

Long-Range Planning and Evaluation

Pages 70–71 show two sample long-range plans.

Long-range planning helps you to implement curriculum goals over time. Think about your program as you read over the lists of goals for children and families, and consider the following questions:

What goals do you want to work on over the next month?

_____

_____

_____

_____

What strategies will help you reach these goals?

_____

_____

_____

_____

What can you do to make sure that you are on track?

_____

_____

_____

_____

How will you evaluate how well your plan worked?

_____

_____

_____

_____

_____

What will you do if you find that your plan needs some changes?

_____

_____

_____

_____

_____

How will you decide which goals to work on next?

_____

_____

_____

_____

_____

Short-Range Planning and Evaluation

Short-range planning helps you to think about what you do day by day, week by week. Your short-range plans help you accomplish your long-range plans.

The sample plan on page 74 of the Curriculum shows how one provider decided to focus on helping children learn about their feelings.

Take a look at the goals in your long-range plan (see your response to the first question on page 50). Then, use the *Weekly Planning Form* on page 329 in Appendix B to make and carry out plans for the next week that will help you meet them.

In what ways does your plan address your goals?

_____

_____

_____

_____

_____

_____

How will you know when you've met your goals?

_____

_____

_____

_____

_____

_____

Creating a Daily Schedule

Infants and toddlers need a schedule that is regular enough to be predictable, yet flexible enough to meet their individual needs.

Describe your daily schedule.

Check to see that your schedule includes the parts listed on page 75.

_____

_____

_____

_____

_____

_____

_____

Think about two children in your program.

How do you individualize the schedule to meet both their needs?

The younger the children in your program, the more individualized a schedule needs to be. Pages 77–78 show how to do this.

_____

_____

_____

_____

_____

_____

_____

Individualizing for Children and Families

Each child and family comes to your program with unique, distinct strengths, needs, and interests. "Individualizing" means making sure your program's goals and objectives meet the needs of each child and family.

Chapter

6

pages 81–100

Individualizing Goals and Objectives for Children

No two infants or toddlers are alike. For this reason, you need to find out about each child's stage of development. Then you can make decisions about how best to promote that child's development.

Choose a particular child in your program. Appendix B includes forms for *Individualizing Goals and Objectives for Young Infants, Mobile Infants, and Toddlers.* Choose the appropriate form for the child you have in mind and fill it out.

See pages 83–86 for an example of how one provider completed the form on a toddler.

What are two important things you learned about this child?

Systematically Observing Children to Get to Know Them as Individuals

When you observe you look at the child from the outside to try to understand what is happening on the inside. Through observing you can learn about a child's family and culture, temperament, special interests, likes and dislikes, behavioral challenges, and learning style.

Do you observe the children in your program regularly (daily, weekly, etc.)? If so, how does observing help you in your work?

_____

_____

_____

_____

Page 88 lists some obstacles to observing on a regular basis— and some proposed solutions.

If your answer to the above question is "No," what steps can you take to observe more regularly?

_____

_____

_____

_____

See pages 87–92 for a discussion of observation and examples of anec-dotal records and running records.

Choose a child to observe for the next two weeks. Complete at least four anecdotal records and two running records.

Putting It All Together: Using the *Planning Form for Individualizing*

After you observe, you use the information you've gathered to make a plan. The *Planning Form for Individualizing* will help you do this. Fill out this form for the child you have observed.

See Appendix B, pages 343–344. Make a copy of this form to plan for each child.

What have you learned about this child which makes him or her unique?

_____

_____

_____

_____

_____

How can you individualize the curriculum to help this child be more successful?

_____

_____

_____

_____

_____

_____

_____

Using the *Goals for Working with Families* Form

See Appendix B, pages 345–348. Make a copy of this form to help you assess your work with each family you serve.

To serve a child well, you must also serve the child's family. Take time to review the *Goals for Working with Families* form. Fill out the form for the family of the child you have been observing.

Which goals do you think you have been effective in meeting?

_____

_____

_____

_____

_____

What areas need your attention?

_____

_____

_____

_____

_____

What steps can you take to strengthen your work with this family?

_____

_____

_____

_____

_____

Creating a Welcoming Environment

The environment you create affects how you, the children, and their families feel and act. It should be a place where you enjoy working with children and where the children and their families feel safe and comfortable.

pages 101–118

Picture your favorite space. What does it look like?

_____

_____

_____

_____

How do you feel when you are in this space?

_____

_____

_____

In what ways does your child care setting contain the same characteristics?

_____

_____

_____

_____

_____

_____

Planning a Responsive Environment

The environment you create must change to meet the changing needs of infants and toddlers.

See the chart on page 102 to help you get started.

How does your environment support the development of the children in your care?

_____

_____

_____

_____

_____

_____

Arranging the Environment
to Give Positive Messages

Pages 103–104 give several examples. You will probably think of many others.

Your environment sends powerful messages to the children and families you serve. Jot down some ways your home or center space sends the following messages:

"This place is comfortable."

_____

_____

_____

_____

"You belong here."

_____

_____

_____

_____

"This is a place you can trust."

_____

_____

_____

_____

"You can explore on your own."

_____

_____

_____

_____

"I will take care of you."

_____

_____

_____

_____

Defining Play Areas Outdoors

It is good for children—and for you—to spend some time outdoors every day. The outdoors offers a whole new environment for infants and toddlers to explore and experience.

Some suggestions are listed on pages 109–110.

How do you provide outdoor spaces for young infants to look around and take in the action?

_____

_____

_____

_____

How does your outdoor space enable mobile infants to cruise and crawl and pull themselves up as they explore the outdoors?

_____

_____

_____

_____

What equipment and materials do you have in your outdoor space to encourage toddlers to run, climb, jump, push, pull, haul, and dump as they actively explore the outdoors?

_____

_____

_____

_____

_____

Selecting and Organizing Materials

The materials you select and display for children make your environment an interesting place to explore and learn. Take a few minutes to look over the toys and materials you have set out.

What do you have available:

to promote fine motor skills?

_____

_____

_____

_____

to promote gross motor skills?

_____

_____

_____

_____

to encourage children to use their senses?

_____

_____

_____

_____

What do you have available:

to inspire dramatic play?

_____

_____

_____

_____

to encourage children to explore shape, size, and balance?

_____

_____

_____

_____

to invite quiet, peaceful play?

_____

_____

_____

_____

to engage children in cooking?

_____

_____

_____

_____

What toys and materials would you like to add to what you have now?

See the list on pages 111–112 for additional ideas.

_____

_____

_____

_____

_____

_____

_____

Adapting the Environment for Children with Special Needs

Children with special needs can often use the materials and take part in activities you already offer if you make a few simple changes.

See pages 113–115 for suggestions that may apply to your situation.

If you have a child or children with special needs in your program, what changes have you made?

_____

_____

_____

_____

_____

_____

_____

Including Children's Families and Cultures in the Environment

Suggestions of positive messages for families can be found on pages 115–116.

Your environment is also for families. If you want family members to feel welcome and valued, it's important to look at your setting through their eyes.

If you were a parent visiting your program for the first time, what messages would you get?

_____

_____

_____

_____

How does your setting reflect the cultural backgrounds of the families you serve?

_____

_____

_____

_____

What changes might you make to help families feel more welcome?

_____

_____

_____

_____

Ensuring Children's Safety

Quality programs keep children safe. Parents—and children—depend on you to prevent accidents as well as to know what to do in an emergency. As children grow and change you can begin to teach them how to keep themselves safe. And you must always balance concerns for children's safety with their need to explore and take risks.

Chapter

8

pages 119–132

What does keeping children safe have to do with helping children develop trust?

_____

_____

_____

_____

_____

_____

Safety Procedures and the Developmental Needs of Children

As children become more mobile, the steps you take to keep them safe must change. Think about a child in your program.

List some of the characteristics that describe this child's development, personality, and interests.

_____

_____

_____

_____

_____

Based on the information you listed, what are some possible safety concerns for this child?

_____

_____

_____

_____

_____

Review the charts on pages 120–121 for examples of developmental characteristics and how you can keep children safe.

What steps might you take to keep this child safe?

_____

_____

_____

_____

_____

Preventing Accidents

If you take time to think about what causes accidents, you can often take measures to keep them from happening. In the space below, draw a picture of your environment to show what you have done to prevent accidents.

Review the list on pages 122–123 of measures to prevent accidents. Then, if you have not already done so, complete the safety checklist on pages 349–356. Are you doing everything that you can to have a safe program? List below any additional safety measures you need to put into place, the steps you will take to do so, and the dates when they are completed.

Safety Measures I Need to Put in Place	Steps to Take	Date Completed

Planning for and Responding to Emergencies

When an emergency happens, it's hard to think clearly. This is why it's so important to have a plan in place that you can follow almost automatically.

Review your program's evacuation plan. If you don't have such a plan, create one and write it below. Try out this plan and see if it works.

For a sample plan, see page 127.

Evacuation plan:

_____

_____

_____

_____

_____

_____

_____

_____

_____

_____

Post your plan where it can be seen easily. Go over the plan with co-workers and parents. If someone's first language is not English, have the plan translated into the appropriate language. During an emergency, it is important that everyone be able to understand what to do and where to go.

Do you conduct regular (at least every month) drills to practice evacuating your space? If not, set up a schedule and begin to do so. Afterwards, reflect on the drill.

Did you observe any procedures that need to be changed? If so, what changes will you make?

_____

_____

_____

_____

_____

Practice your evacuation plan until it becomes automatic for you and the children.

Helping Children to Become Aware of Safety

See pages 128–129 for strategies to help children learn to keep themselves safe.

When you create a safe environment and take steps to prevent accidents, you help children learn about safety. You also help children take the first steps toward becoming responsible for their own safety.

What safety rules do you have in your program?

_____

_____

_____

_____

How well do you think the children in your program are able to understand and follow the rules?

_____

_____

_____

_____

_____

_____

Knowing it's difficult for infants and toddlers to follow rules, what steps do you take to keep them safe?

_____

_____

_____

_____

_____

_____

Balancing Concerns for Children's Safety with Their Need for Exploration

Children need us to help keep them safe. At the same time, they need to explore and take reasonable risks. Your challenge is to find a balance. Take a few minutes to explore your feelings and practices about this issue.

See pages 129–130 for further discussion about this topic.

Do children feel free to explore the indoor and outdoor environments in your program?

_____
_____
_____
_____
_____
_____
_____

Do the children find your environment challenging?

_____
_____
_____
_____
_____
_____
_____

How do you encourage children to take "reasonable" risks?

_____
_____
_____
_____
_____
_____
_____

Promoting Children's Health

When children are healthy they have the energy to explore and learn. Keeping infants and toddlers healthy is a big job. Their health and nutritional needs will change as they get older. This chapter discusses how you can prevent health problems and respond to sick children. It tells you what to do if you suspect child abuse or neglect and how you can help children develop good health habits as they grow.

pages 133–150

 Good health gives you the energy to care for children. Eating a good diet and getting enough sleep and exercise are three ways you take care of yourself.

In what ways do you promote your own good health?

_____

_____

_____

_____

_____

_____

_____

_____

_____

Meeting Children's Health Requirements from Birth to Age Three

Review the charts on pages 134–136.

As with safety, when children grow, the steps you take to keep them healthy must change. Think about a child in your program. (It does not have to be the same child you focused on earlier.)

How would you describe this child's development, personality, and interests?

_____

_____

_____

_____

_____

Based on your knowledge of this child, what are your health concerns?

_____

_____

_____

_____

What steps can you take to keep this child healthy?

_____

_____

_____

_____

Preventing Health Problems

Screening is a first step in preventing health problems. In addition, all children need to be immunized against preventable diseases such as measles, chicken pox, and mumps. The Centers for Disease Control and the American Academy of Pediatrics publish an immunization schedule for infants and toddlers.

See Appendix D for the immunization schedule as of January 1995 for children under age three. Be sure to check for updates, as recommendations are subject to change.

How do you record and track children's immunizations in your program?

_____

_____

_____

Check the health records of the children in your care. Are they all up to date? If not, what are your responsibilities?

_____

_____

_____

How do you decide which records should be available to all who care for the child and which should be confidential?

_____

_____

_____

Checking for Good Health Practices in Your Program

See Appendix C, pages 357–362.

Use the checklist in the Curriculum to help you identify whether you are doing everything you can to keep children healthy. In the chart below, list any practices you need to put in place, the steps you will take to do so, and the date you complete each step.

Health Practices I Need to Put in Place	Steps to Take	Date Completed

Responding to Child Abuse and Neglect

As difficult as it can be to accept, child abuse and neglect are facts of life. According to the law, if you suspect a child in your care is being abused, you *must* report it.

See pages 140–141 for a definition of abuse and neglect and behaviors that indicate a child may be abused or neglected.

What is your program's written policy for reporting suspected abuse? (If you do not have one, it is critical that you develop one.)

_____

_____

_____

_____

_____

_____

_____

What is your legal responsibility?

Find out what the law in your state requires and who you report to if you suspect child abuse or neglect.

_____

_____

_____

_____

_____

_____

_____

Responding to Sick Children

No matter how careful you are, children get sick. Therefore, every program should have policies about what to do.

How do you feel about caring for a sick child in your program?

_____

_____

_____

_____

Pages 142–143 discuss caring for children who are temporarily ill.

How do you care for a sick child without neglecting the other children in your program?

_____

_____

_____

_____

A reasonable, clear policy lets parents and caregivers/ teachers know what is expected ahead of time.

What is your program's policy on when sick children should be kept home?

_____

_____

_____

_____

Helping Children Develop Good Nutrition and Other Health Habits

With your help, infants and toddlers can take their first steps in learning to keep themselves healthy.

What do children learn about keeping healthy by watching you each day?

_____

_____

_____

_____

_____

_____

_____

What do you do to help children learn and use self-help skills to promote their own good health?

Page 147 includes a list of strategies that may give you additional ideas.

_____

_____

_____

_____

_____

_____

_____

Using Partnerships to Enhance Children's Health

See page 148 for a list of places to go in your community for support.

You protect children's health best when you are a partner with their families and community agencies.

What are some of the specific ways you work with families or community resources to keep children healthy?

_____

_____

_____

_____

_____

_____

_____

_____

Guiding Children's Behavior

Children need us to guide them—to help·them learn what is acceptable behavior and what is not. Often, how we respond to children is shaped by how we were treated when we were young.

pages 151–164

How were you disciplined as a child?

_____

_____

_____

How do your experiences affect the way you discipline or guide children today?

_____

_____

_____

What is your goal in guiding children's behavior—what do you want them to learn?

_____

_____

_____

Taking a Positive Approach

See pages 151–152 for examples of each of these behaviors.

A positive approach to guiding children's behavior means helping children learn self-control and how to relate to others in caring ways.

Describe a time you stopped a dangerous behavior.

_____

_____

_____

Describe a time you prevented dangerous behavior.

_____

_____

_____

Describe a time you redirected a child's behavior.

_____

_____

_____

How did your actions provide positive guidance and help children develop self-discipline?

_____

_____

_____

_____

Guiding the Behavior of Young Infants, Mobile Infants, and Toddlers

How you guide a child's behavior depends largely on the child's age and temperament. Because children change so rapidly during their first three years, the strategies that you use to guide their behavior must change too.

Work with one or more colleagues to brainstorm three strategies for guiding the behavior of children in each age group.

The suggestions on pages 152–154 may be helpful.

To guide the behavior of young infants, we

_____

_____

_____

_____

To guide the behavior of mobile infants, we

_____

_____

_____

_____

To guide the behavior of toddlers, we

_____

_____

_____

_____

Responding to Challenging Behaviors

At one time or another children under three are likely to hit, have temper tantrums, or bite. And like many caregivers/teachers you may ask yourself, "What do I do now?" One place to start is to be aware of your own feelings.

How do you feel when a child cries, hits, has a temper tantrum, or bites?

_____

_____

_____

_____

_____

_____

_____

See pages 154–155 for ways of responding to challenging behaviors.

How do you address the child's needs even when the behavior makes you angry or frustrated?

_____

_____

_____

_____

_____

_____

_____

Temper Tantrums

Temper tantrums can be upsetting for everyone.

Describe the last temper tantrum you saw. (Be as specific as you can about what the child did.)

_____

_____

_____

_____

_____

If that child could tell you what he or she was feeling, what do you think the child would say?

See page 156 for one possibility.

_____

_____

_____

_____

_____

_____

Once a tantrum begins, your first concern should be to keep the child from hurting him or herself or someone else. Reassure the child that you are there until the tantrum is over. Try to stay as calm as possible so you can help the child calm down.

The best approach is to try to prevent tantrums.

See page 156 for a discussion of how to prevent tantrums.

Talk with others and record your ideas about ways to prevent temper tantrums by:

minimizing frustration.

_____

_____

_____

_____

giving toddlers plenty of opportunities to feel competent.

_____

_____

_____

_____

giving toddlers a chance to be babies too.

_____

_____

_____

_____

anticipating children's physical needs.

_____

_____

_____

_____

Biting

Anyone who cares for infants and toddlers has experienced the problem of biting. If you can identify the reasons why a child bites, you can often come up with effective strategies to prevent it.

The chart on page 157 identifies some typical situations when children tend to bite and strategies to help prevent biting.

What do your program's guidelines on biting tell you to do? (If your program doesn't have guidelines, now is the time to develop them.)

_____

_____

_____

_____

_____

_____

It is helpful to think ahead about how you will respond to a child who bites. On pages 158–159 you will find a list of suggested steps to take. Read this list and adapt it as necessary for your use.

You may want to share this information with families in a parent handbook or during a parent meeting—preferably before an incident occurs.

One common response to biting is to "bite the child back."

Why is this not an appropriate response?

_____

_____

_____

_____

_____

_____

Helping Children Relate Positively
to Each Other

Children learn about relating to others by how others care for them. When you treat children in loving and consistent ways and show how much you respect them, you teach them "prosocial behavior."

What might children learn from watching you relate to others?

_____

_____

_____

_____

The list on pages 160–161 describes things you can do each day to help children learn to get along with each other.

List four other strategies you use in your program to promote prosocial behavior.

_____

_____

_____

_____

Give three examples from your program of infants or toddlers relating positively to other children.

_____

_____

_____

_____

_____

Part III Routines

Day by Day

Many adults do routines on auto-pilot. While they may be boring to an adult, to an infant or toddler, they are important events. Routines are times to give children individual attention and meet basic needs. They are predictable, yet they vary enough to hold children's attention and interest. The younger the child, the more time you will spend in the daily routines of hellos and good-byes, diapering and toileting, eating and mealtimes, sleeping and napping, and getting dressed. Part III describes each of these routines and shows how you can turn these "have-to-do" activities into opportunities to build relationships and promote children's learning.

Hellos and Good-byes

The Creative Curriculum for Infants & Toddlers encourages you to take time saying hellos and good-byes. Focusing on these routines allows you to take advantage of the rich learning opportunities they offer.

pages 169–178

Learning to separate from and reunite with people we love is a lifelong process that brings out deep feelings in everyone. Remember some times you said hello or good-bye to someone you love.

What strategies have you yourself used to make hellos and good-byes easier?

_____

_____

_____

_____

How do you think parents feel about saying good-bye to their children in the morning and hello again in the afternoon?

_____

_____

_____

_____

_____

Observe one child carefully during hellos and good-byes over a week's time.

See pages 174–176 for further information on this topic.

What do you think the child is feeling?

_____

_____

_____

_____

_____

You can use ideas from Chapter 11 and the letter to families to help you get started.

Talk with members of that child's family about what you observed.

What do they think their child is experiencing?

_____

_____

_____

_____

_____

Discuss ways that you and the family can support the child to make these times easier. List the steps you will take.

_____

_____

_____

_____

_____

_____

Diapering
and Toileting

Though there are times you—and parents—will want and need to hurry through diapering, the time you spend changing a child can help strengthen your relationship with that child. With your support and attention, diapering and toileting can be positive learning experiences. Eventually (typically around age two-and-a-half) children—much to the delight of their parents and caregivers/ teachers—are ready to begin using the toilet and do so.

Chapter

12

pages 179–190

If you care for children who are not yet toilet trained, how many diapers do you estimate that you change a day? Each week? Each month? Each year?

_____

_____

What memories from your past do you think may influence your approach to diapering and toileting?

_____

_____

_____

_____

_____

_____

_____

How do you stay calm and cheerful as you help children learn to use the toilet?

_____

_____

_____

_____

Because children need help in learning to use the toilet at home and in child care, it is important that you keep in touch with families about their expectations, feelings, and about what is happening in both settings.

How and when do you talk with parents about diapering and toileting?

_____

_____

_____

What information do you share?

_____

_____

_____

What additional information do you need and how will you get it?

_____

_____

_____

Eating and Mealtimes

Mealtimes and related activities—such as setting the table, washing hands, talking together, and brushing teeth—give children opportunities to develop self-help skills as well as communication and social skills. Mealtimes are also times to practice fine motor skills—holding a cup, picking up finger foods—and to develop good nutrition and health habits.

Chapter

13

pages 191–200

Think back to when you were a child.

What were mealtimes like in your family?

_____

_____

_____

_____

_____

In what ways are mealtimes in your program similar or different?

_____

_____

_____

_____

_____

Over the next day or two, step back and look at mealtimes in your program from the point of view of a young infant, a mobile infant, or a toddler.

What kinds of experiences do you think this child is having during mealtimes?

_____

_____

_____

_____

_____

What makes mealtimes for this child an opportunity to learn and be social?

_____

_____

_____

_____

_____

See the strategies on pages 194–196 for suggestions on how to organize mealtimes and promote children's independence.

Based on your observations, what changes might you make so that mealtimes are more relaxing and enjoyable?

_____

_____

_____

_____

_____

Families have different traditions and practices related to mealtimes. Young children will feel more at home in your program if you learn about these practices and use them.

Ask several families to describe mealtimes in their homes and how they make these times enjoyable. Discuss the foods children eat and what kind of assistance, if any, they require.

How can you use what you learned from families to make mealtimes in child care familiar and pleasant for children?

_____

_____

_____

_____

_____

_____

_____

Families are eager to hear from you as well.

How do you share information about mealtimes?

_____

_____

_____

_____

_____

_____

To help children learn during mealtimes, you have to take time to observe what each child is doing, think about what the child may be experiencing, and then figure out how to respond. How you respond to a young infant will be different from what you would say or do with a mobile infant or a toddler.

Review the charts on pages 196-197 to help you get started.

Over the next week, make a point of observing carefully during mealtimes and keep a record of what children do and how you respond.

What the Child Did	How I Responded

Sleeping and Naptime

Naptime is an important time of day for children—and for you. It gives children the rest they need or, if they do not sleep, a break from group life. It gives you quiet time when you can relax, meet with colleagues or parents, and refocus your attention and energy so you can be more available to children. Children learn to trust their world and themselves as they discover that child care is a safe place in which to relax and sleep.

pages 201–212

What was bedtime like for you as a child? Did you have goodnight rituals such as reading a story or having your back rubbed as your parents sang a song? Or was bedtime a battle of wills? How did it make you feel?

Write about what you remember.

_____

_____

_____

_____

_____

_____

_____

_____

_____

_____

Chapter 14 has suggestions for creating a restful environment and dealing with a crying child.

Naptime in child care settings can be a challenge since it involves helping so many children sleep. Infants sleep on individual schedules. It often seems that the moment one falls asleep, another wakes up. As the older children become more tired and cranky and adults become more desperate for a break, the greater the potential for tension and conflict around sleeping.

No matter how knowledgeable or skilled you are, count on the fact that there will be days when a child(ren) will not sleep.

See the list on page 203 for additional ideas.

Why do you think some children find it difficult to sleep? If you could put yourself in their place at naptime, what do you think they might be thinking about?

_____

_____

_____

_____

_____

You may want to ask parents what they do at home. Also, see the list on pages 205–206 for additional ideas.

What do you do when a child doesn't sleep? How do you balance the needs of the individual with the needs of the group?

_____

_____

_____

_____

_____

As with every routine, working with parents as partners makes things better for everyone. Children get the benefit of continuity between home and child care. You and their families get the information you need to make sleeping and naptime a positive experience for children.

What kinds of information about sleep patterns do you and families share each day?

_____

_____

_____

_____

_____

_____

_____

What are some things you have learned from families about helping their child get to sleep?

_____

_____

_____

_____

_____

_____

_____

_____

What do you think families may have learned from you?

_____

_____

_____

_____

_____

_____

_____

_____

Getting Dressed

Dressing offers pleasant—and at times challenging—moments with infants and toddlers. When you stop to think about it, dressing is quite a complicated activity.

Think back to what you had to do to dress yourself this morning.

Chapter

15

pages 213–220

What different skills did you need?

_____

_____

_____

_____

Through experience, children learn to snap snaps, tug up zippers, open and close buttons, pull a shirt on and off over their heads, and choose clothes that please them and suit the weather.

How do you help children feel competent about dressing— even though you have to help them a lot?

See the list on page 214 for additional ideas.

_____

_____

_____

_____

_____

_____

As children become more mobile, getting dressed can become stressful. Children must stop what they are doing, be held in place, and turn over control of their body to someone else.

Imagine you are a mobile infant—or toddler—happily climbing over a bunch of big pillows in the middle of the room. Suddenly, your caregiver/teacher asks you to sit down on the bench and begins pushing your foot into your boot so you can go outdoors. Someone bigger has interrupted you and controls what you do.

If you were that child, how would you respond?

_____

_____

_____

_____

_____

_____

How do you handle a mobile infant or toddler who protests getting dressed?

_____

_____

_____

_____

_____

_____

Talk with a child's family member about how they handle similar protests. Write down what you learn.

_____

_____

_____

_____

_____

_____

_____

Part
IV Activities
Day by Day

As children mature and acquire new
skills and interests, you will
be focusing more of
your planning time
on activities. When
we speak of activities
for infants and toddlers,
we do not mean planning
an activity for a specific
time of day, gathering materials,
introducing the activity to a group, and conducting it through to completion.
We believe activities are integrated into everything you do throughout the day.
When you feed an infant, for example, and allow her to mush the carrots on
her tray, you are providing a "preparing and tasting food" activity. When you
sing with a toddler and take giant steps on your way to a nearby park you are
"having fun with music and movement." As children grow older, there will, of
course, be times when you offer planned activities, yet these should always be
only one of many experiences available to children at any given time.

In Part IV, we look at eight activities: playing with toys, dabbling in art, imitating
and pretending, enjoying stories and books, tasting and preparing food,
exploring sand and water, having fun with music and movement, and going
outdoors.

Playing with Toys

Toys teach. They teach skills and concepts as children play and have fun. Young infants explore toys by holding them and putting them in their mouths. As a result, everything you provide must be very clean and safe. Mobile infants love balls and toys they can push and pull, fill and dump, and bang. And toddlers with their growing skills enjoy a range of toys they can use to pretend, to build, to put together, and to throw.

Chapter
16

pages 225–238

What was your favorite toy as a young child? Why did you like this toy so much?

_____

_____

_____

_____

_____

How do you give the children in your program an experience similar to the one you just described?

_____

_____

_____

_____

_____

Over the next week, observe the infants and toddlers in your care.

Which toys do they most often choose?

_____

_____

_____

_____

What makes these toys appealing and fun for the children?

_____

_____

_____

Are there any toys that the children do not use? Why do you think this is so?

_____

_____

_____

How often do you add new toys and put others away? What happens when you do this?

_____

_____

_____

What you say and do as children play with toys lets them know you care about them and are excited about what they can do. You also promote their learning.

You can find suggestions of what to say to young infants, mobile infants, and toddlers on pages 234–235.

In the chart below, record five things you said to an infant or toddler playing with a toy. Next to your comments, write down what you hoped the child would learn.

What I Said	What I Wanted the Child to Learn

Dabbling in Art

Art is much more than coloring or painting. It is part of our daily lives—and children's too. When an infant looks at and reaches out to touch your nubby blue sweater and a toddler notices sunlight peeping through the clouds after a rain shower, they are experiencing art. Art experiences are important for even very young children. As children grow they can use art materials to express their ideas and creativity.

pages 239–252

What kinds of art experiences do you offer the infants and toddlers in your program?

_____

_____

_____

_____

_____

_____

_____

The daily experiences you provide for young infants—touching soft objects, smearing their hands in pudding, watching colorful mobiles—introduce them to art. Mobile infants will love dabbling in finger paint, squeezing playdough, and making marks with crayons. Toddlers can paint with objects like brushes and sponges, mold clay or playdough, print with stamps, and paste.

See pages 240–243 and 246–249 for additional ideas.

Plan an art experience for the infants or toddlers in your program. Select one of the activities in the Curriculum, or make up one of your own.

Try it out. Observe what children do and record your observations below.

_____

_____

_____

_____

_____

Pages 246–249 discuss a variety of strategies for encouraging children's involvement in art activities.

What did you say or do during the art activity to encourage the children to explore and enjoy the experience?

_____

_____

_____

_____

What, if anything, would you do differently next time?

_____

_____

_____

_____

_____

If you work with mobile infants or toddlers, make one of the art recipes in the Curriculum. Put it out and observe how children use this art material.

See pages 240–243 for these recipes.

Use the space below to record what happens.

_____

_____

_____

_____

_____

_____

_____

_____

_____

_____

_____

If you work with toddlers, try varying the activity by putting out some props or tools for playing with the art material and note how children respond.

See suggestions on pages 247–250.

_____

_____

_____

_____

_____

_____

_____

_____

_____

Would you use this recipe again? Why or why not?

_____

_____

_____

_____

_____

_____

_____

_____

_____

What would you like families to know about this art experience?

_____

_____

_____

_____

_____

_____

_____

_____

_____

Imitating and Pretending

Pretend play is one important way that young children come to understand the world around them. You have probably seen young infants imitating the actions of others. True pretend play—for example, holding a doll and feeding it make-believe food or crawling around and barking like a dog—typically begins to appear between a child's first and second birthdays.

Chapter

18

pages 253–264

Think back to when you were a child. What kinds of pretend play did you enjoy?

_____

_____

_____

_____

_____

_____

What were your favorite props for pretend play?

_____

_____

_____

_____

_____

See the suggestions on pages 254–256 for some ideas.

What materials do you have available for infants and toddlers to encourage imitation and pretend play?

_____

_____

_____

_____

_____

_____

_____

_____

_____

_____

Make a point to observe the infants and toddlers you work with to identify examples of imitation and pretend play.

What did you discover?

_____

_____

_____

_____

_____

_____

_____

_____

_____

_____

Language development is closely connected to pretend play. Therefore, what you say to a child is very important. Your attention and encouragement will inspire pretend play more than any other factor.

What might you talk about with a young infant to promote language development?

On pages 256–257 you will find some examples of what you might say to a young infant or mobile infant.

_____

_____

_____

_____

_____

_____

_____

_____

_____

What might you talk about with a mobile infant who is learning to imitate?

_____

_____

_____

_____

_____

_____

_____

_____

_____

_____

_____

On pages 258–259 are examples of pretend play in toddlers.

If you work with toddlers, pick one child to observe for several days. Note examples of pretend play and what you do or say to encourage this child's imaginative play.

What I Observed	What I Said to Encourage Imaginative Play

Enjoying Stories and Books

Infants and toddlers usually love to sit in your lap and listen as you read to them. Even very young infants who do not yet understand the meaning of words will enjoy looking at a book. It's never too early to introduce infants and toddlers to stories, poems, and books.

pages 265–276

Do you remember being read to as a child? What positive memories do you have about the experience?

In the space below, jot down some ideas about how you can provide the children in your program with positive feelings about books.

Which books do the children in your care seem to enjoy most?

_____

_____

_____

_____

_____

_____

_____

_____

_____

_____

_____

Why do you think these books are their favorites?

_____

_____

_____

_____

_____

_____

_____

_____

_____

_____

_____

Infants and toddlers love books about themselves. Do you have any homemade books in your program? Try making one about the children and sharing it with them.

A homemade book can be very simple—just photos of children and their families. See page 268 for information.

Record their reactions in the space below.

_____

_____

_____

_____

_____

_____

_____

Observe someone reading to a child or small group of children. For example, you might invite a colleague or a parent to read, or visit your local library during a storytime session.

How did this person make story reading enjoyable for the children?

_____

_____

_____

_____

_____

_____

_____

See pages 270–272, "Enjoying Stories and Books with Children" for additional suggestions.

From observing this person and what you have read in the Curriculum, what new ideas do you want to try with your children?

Tasting and Preparing Food

Tasting and preparing food are part of everyday living with infants and toddlers. They feel proud and important when they can help with the real work of preparing the food they eat—for example, by scrubbing a carrot or dipping a cracker into yogurt.

Chapter

20

pages 277–286

How do you involve children in food preparation activities?

What do you do to make food preparation with mobile infants and toddlers an enjoyable and successful experience for all?

See page 280 for suggestions of ways to make food activities a successful experience.

How do you ensure that food activities are safe and healthy?

Page 278 discusses the topic.

Children's families can give you ideas for food preparation activities. This may be a way to bring their cultures into your program.

What ideas have you learned from the families in your program?

_____

_____

_____

_____

_____

_____

_____

Additional ideas are listed on pages 281–283. You can also look at books on cooking with children. Three are listed on page 283.

The best food preparation experiences for mobile infants and toddlers are ones that allow them to be active. For example, children can shake, dip, mix, squeeze, spread, and beat. Try out some food preparation activities suggested in *The Creative Curriculum for Infants & Toddlers.*

Keep a list of what children do and how they respond.

_____

_____

_____

_____

_____

_____

Exploring Sand and Water

Infants and toddlers are naturally attracted to sand and water. The magic of splashing water and digging into sand appeals to almost everyone. However, because even toddlers may get sand in their mouths, it should be sterile. For this same reason, sand play is best left to older infants and toddlers.

pages 287–296

What memories do you have of playing in sand and water?

_____

_____

_____

_____

Ironically, many caregivers/teachers feel a sense of dread rather than pleasure when they think of sand and water play for infants and toddlers. One big concern is mess. Let's reflect on this.

Observe a child in your program freely playing in sand and water. What do you suppose the experience is like for this child?

_____

_____

_____

_____

What would the experience be like if you were constantly saying, "Don't splash" or "Don't spill?"

_____

_____

_____

_____

Review the list on pages 289–290 for additional ideas and talk with parents and colleagues.

What steps can you take to control messes while letting this child—and the others—enjoy sand and water?

_____

_____

_____

See pages 290–291 for ideas.

If you work with mobile infants and toddlers, think about some new props you might offer them to use with sand or water. Collect a few and try them out.

How did the children use the props?

_____

_____

_____

_____

What did you say and do to promote their sand and water play?

_____

_____

Having Fun with Music and Movement

Music and movement are a natural part of children's lives. A newborn is comforted by the rhythmic sound of her parent's heartbeat as she is held close. Toddlers love to bang on pots and pans with spoons and "dance" to the beat. And now we know that music has a role in brain development. Listening to and repeating rhymes, songs, and chants help "wire" a child's brain for learning.

Chapter

22

pages 297–306

What kinds of music do you enjoy listening to or creating?

_____

_____

_____

_____

_____

What role does music play in your life?

_____

_____

_____

_____

_____

Whether or not you can sing or dance, you can share music and movement with children. Your ability to enjoy them and have fun is far more important than your skills.

The list on pages 299–301 may offer you more ideas to try.

What kinds of music and movement experiences do you do with children?

_____

_____

_____

_____

See pages 301–304 for ideas.

Observe the children you work with as you engage them in music and movement activities.

How do you know they are enjoying themselves?

_____

_____

_____

What do you do to help infants or toddlers have fun with music and movement?

_____

_____

_____

Families can be a great resource for music at your program. Including their families' music in your program is a good way to celebrate children's cultures.

Ask families to bring in music you can play, dance to, or sing with children. Or even better, invite family members to share their family songs and/or dances with children in your setting.

Going Outdoors

Going outdoors is fun for children. It is a healthy change for them—and for you—to be in an open space and close to nature.

Think about what you liked to do outdoors as a child.

pages 307–318

Describe your two favorite activities and what you especially enjoyed about each one.

_____

_____

_____

_____

_____

_____

_____

How can you offer the same kinds of experiences you had to infants and toddlers?

_____

_____

_____

_____

_____

_____

For additional suggestions about keeping children safe and healthy outdoors, see pages 308–310.

Go back to Appendix E: Safety and Health Checklist (pages 349–362) and see if this helps you to pinpoint any areas of concern.

Look around your outdoor space(s) with an eye for safety and health hazards. Think of the children in your care. What health or safety hazards might they discover as they explore and play?

In the chart below, list the hazards you identify, then describe the steps you will take to address each one, and the date you completed it.

Outdoor Safety/Heath Hazards	Steps to Take	Date Completed

Think of a particular child in your program.

What are some outdoor experiences this child enjoys that enable him or her to:

See pages 311– 314 for additional examples of how children learn through outdoor play.

have sensory explorations?

_____

_____

_____

_____

_____

engage in gross motor play?

_____

_____

_____

_____

_____

do fine motor play?

_____

_____

_____

_____

_____

In *The Creative Curriculum for Infants & Toddlers,* we describe many different outdoor experiences for infants and toddlers. Select two that are new to you and try them with your infants and toddlers.

Use the space below to note what happens.

Reflecting on Your Professional Development

We hope that using this Journal has helped you to appreciate the wealth of information you have about infants and toddlers and their families.

What strengths did you discover about yourself as you worked through the Journal?

_____

_____

_____

_____

_____

_____

_____

What strengths did you discover about your program?

_____

_____

_____

_____

_____

_____

What challenges did the Journal help you address?

_____

_____

_____

_____

_____

_____

What questions, if any, do you still have about using *The Creative Curriculum for Infants & Toddlers?*

_____

_____

_____

_____

_____

_____

Refer back to Part I of the Curriculum for ideas on getting ongoing support.

What steps can you take to get answers to your questions and to continue your professional development?

_____

_____

_____

_____

_____

_____

Closing Thoughts

As we close, go back to the map you made of your Professional Journey at the start of the Journal (see page 6). As a result of having completed this Journal, does your map take on new meaning? If you think changes/additions are in order, make them using a different colored pen.

Since caring for infants and toddlers is an ongoing journey, you'll probably want to go back and reflect on what you have written here at a later time, say six months from now. As you look over what you wrote, think about what you were doing at the time that made you feel this way. See if you still feel the same, or if some of your ideas have changed.

Good caregiving and teaching never stay the same. New ideas and experiences make us rethink a particular position or—just as likely—reconfirm our original thoughts. Go back from time to time to revisit your Journal. Use it as a starting point to keep you thinking about infant and toddler care. Today's thoughts will spark new ideas for tomorrow. And in the course of your journey, you will become an increasingly skillful caregiver/teacher.